Habanero Love

A Poem of Sacred Passion

Habanero Love

A Poem of Sacred Passion

Jaiya John

Soul Water Rising

Camarillo, California

Printed in the United States of America

Soul Water Rising
Camarillo, California
http://www.soulwater.org

Library of Congress Control Number: 2014902142
ISBN 978-0-9916401-5-7

First Soul Water Rising Edition, Softcover: 2016

Poetry / Romance / Spirituality

Editors:
Jacqueline V. Richmond
Kent W. Mortensen

Cover & Interior Design: Jaiya John
Cover Photo: © Jaiya John

Coffee and Love taste best when hot.

—Ethiopian Proverb

We began nakedly,
with the searing passion
of spices and peppers,

on cutting boards,
under cold running water,
in virgin oil on cast iron heat.

Rinsing bell peppers to Latin music,
Spanish guitar inflaming our temperature.

Slicing fiery habaneros to the cadence
of sensuous, aromatic drumbeats.

Piano punctuating jalapeños roasting.
Saxophone sautéing robust garlic cloves,

pungent yellow onion, fresh cut basil,
organic oregano, pimentos bright.

Moonlight and candlelight.

Cayenne and cumin.
Sea salt surrender.

My hands soon gently

on your glory hips.

Movement.

Salsa, merengue.
Movement, moonlight.
Flamenco. Fire.

Lips on fingertips well-seasoned.
Black pepper. Crushed coriander.

Thyme and time merging spices
in the black blistering skillet.
In the heat of joining.

We began with a joining.

Sizzling, steam rising,
scent of spices a bravado begging,
overtaking, filling our climate.
Potency, boldness, perspiration.

Slow taste from a finger.

Stirring soulfully, to the music.
To moonlight.

Pulse and throb of peppers popping
in oil no longer virgin.

First taste. Mmmm. Fire.

Sensual evidence of Love made.
Between peppers and spices.

Lips burning. Old yearning.
Beyond this world.

Something supernatural.
Seasoning of Sacredness.

Departing this plane for cloud ranges,
atmospheric meadows.

Higher still.
Bodies gone.
Lucid dreaming.

Something Sacred feeding our souls.

Famished. Finished. Fulfilled.

Stunned and silent.
Evaporated.

Nothing left but the taste and burn
of habanero on the tongue,

drifting like a warm current
down the river of our soul.

We began like this.

Last night,
I gathered in Sacred circle
with my people,

in a dark, mystic sweat lodge
made of memory and breeze.

Sweat was potent, mystic,
magnified beneath the impossible
glowing Circle Moon.

This morning my heart is a swollen river,
overflowing and flooding my soul.

Sacredly, I say these things to you:

Something in your spirit
stirs my ocean floor.

You make my soul cry gratitude.
I am overflowing.

You move my earth.

A deep sea of feeling runs through you,
a steep canyon of empathy filled
with forceful currents.

What is in you
has been in you since ancestry.

It now picks up force
and floods through me.

Wherever you are,
my soul is flying over,

a condor of mist and heartbeat,
wings spread to the horizons,

talons set to serrate the sky
that separates me from you.

I am a cloud, ripe with rain.

Your long drought has a scent
like the skin of desert stones.

Let me fall over you, wet and silent,
and pool in your porous nature.

Let me parachute into your canopy,
with these Love provisions that
cannot expire,

not in the humidity of time,
nor in the aridity of change.

Moments with you have become

my Sacred Lake.

When I am away, I dream of absconding.

As I return, I see that the trees
have grown green in my absence.

In the sunlight of your presence,
those trees glow a magical green of jade.

Air is fragrant with the scent of new
wildflowers. Birds sing a forest chorus.

Fish and turtles quickly greet me.

In my gush of gratitude,
my tears overtake the lake.

I am an explosion of Joy,
on a bank of serenity.

I have found Sacred spaces
over time, in my life.

When the weather is warm enough,
I choose to live in nature's palm, in Beauty.

In winter, I dream of spring, and this
garden coming to life again.

You make me cry. Sweetly.

My Love is truly with you.

It is sharing the blanket
on which you lie, turning pages
of stories whose characters
speak your native tongue.

Your joy at simple pleasures
is a stunning purity,
a particular nectar
that I covet.

I am remembering your birthday,
and the way we spent it.

I can feel the warm breeze
whispering over the golden hills.

What an invitation you extended,
for me to lie with you in the dancing grass.

The champagne and fresh bread,
the meadow, the languorous moments...

My heart was made well.
A paper lantern, light and lifting.

My heart ushers Beauty and Goodness,
and Peace to you today.

This morning, I read your letter,
your ethereal vision of the blanket.

A sensation spread through me,
my heart and soul both drawn open,
wide, wide.

I dissolved into spirit, as pure Love
flowered from within and flooded me.

Love clouds absorbed me.
I succumbed, surrendered
into a crying rain,
a beautiful drowning.

Do not resuscitate.

When I write to you, or read from you,
the sand at the shore of my heart shifts
warmly in the water.

Your words leave me wordless.
Heart-soaked.
Acutely reverent.

Something Divine is at hand.

I am singing a song of Beauty
for your day.

Enlist these homeless notes.

I would Love to share this lake
that is my life with you.

I know you would cherish and thrill
to her subtle secrets and sacred pleasures.

Creation is Loving me
in a blanket of Beauty.

Warm, perfect air. Adoring sunshine.

Water Spirit is making
the most soothing sound,
wave after wave lapping shore.

Very light perfect breeze.
Crystal clear water.

Ladybugs everywhere on the sand,
surrounding me. So much Love.

Sky is powder blue,
faint wisps of white clouds.
Trees line the bay in the distance.

At the mouth of the bay, toward the lake,
the water turns a rich turquoise.

What is this moment but Heaven?
And Love.

I wish you were here.

I have been told of dunes by a lakeshore,
that whisper with a spirit of bears.

I will go there tomorrow
to restore from today,

and to commune with God,
so that tomorrow evening,

I may commune with man.

For in my servitude,
I find and open the time capsule
that holds the Holy papers

on which my name is written
next to your own.

Between our two names,
a two-word proverb says everything:

be with.

Your people are legend for me.
They have yielded a phenomenal soul,
raised a priceless daughter,
endowed a singular treasure.

I must pour libations for them.
I must call out their names.

Wherever your ancestors walk,
that is now my pilgrimage.

What stream they drink from,
is my baptismal water.

They sing your ancestral song.
I will learn it.

It will become my daily ceremony.
My rite of passage.

The Kente cloth you wear
over your fine form

tells many stories.

Tell this one, too.

Weave this thread
of our cauldron colors
into your fabric of generations.

Sew a dress that flows mystically,
an enchanting waterfall.

Be a walking heat wave.

Inspire my soul to the surface
as I walk with you.

Introvert my outward energy.
Then move into me.

Touch me.
Initiate the temblor quake.

Your words and sentiment
are achingly beautiful to me.

I have not ever experienced such
glorious expression,

nor so great a harmony
as your soul's song within my heart.

Your soul voice is precious parchment.

I run for the preserving ointment,
the sealing glass.

You are a dove placed in my palm.

I will keep my hand open,
and raised toward sky.

I pray that you be only free
and filled with Purity and Joy.

I see you there, in that Sweet Land,
exuding your Love and Light
as your legacy to the world.

May you have awakened Beautifully.

May a field of flowers blossom
before your sleepy eyes,

and the possibility of a clear creek

take you in its arms.

I think of you waking,
and I am taken. By a dream of day.

At the lake. You and I.
Air chilled and breezy. Holy.

Woodpecker codes out a Love letter:
so glad you could be here with me today.

As she sleeps, he Loves her.
Blanketing her body
in the warmth of his affection.

As she wakes, he Loves her,
washing her face in the freshwaters
of his tears, washing her spirit clean.

Even as she dreams,

her heart is a harp whose strings
his fingers cannot help but caress.

Her vibration is a music
that moves through his soul,

a flock of cardinals
so radiant and glorious in song.

And so he touches her strings.

She is the opera.
His heart the tenor.

She draws his basso profondo
from its deep burrow.

An Awesome Conductor begs his voice
to fill Creation with an overture of Love.

As she drifts into sleep,

he desires nothing more
than to hold her in his arms,
and give her dreaming heart a home...

With my heart's breath,
I touch your anxiousness away.

A bird is at your window.
Flown from the aviary of my heart
to be with you.

Sweet brook gurgles in the meadow.
New flowers mark their territory fragrantly.

A tree bodyguards a blossom.
Sun shafts spray the mossy soil.
A breeze feathers by.

Lying silently beside all of this, a blanket.
And atop, two hearts
beating tender synchronicity.

Something precious keeps washing
into my heart with the tide.

A sea shell, sand dollar,
necklace of pearls...

All of these the ways Love says,
Here I am. Take me. I am yours.

Love words aren't
good enough anymore.

The Glory I am filled with
can only be painted by Silence.

Overflowing, crying, grateful.
Fulfilled, illuminated, hopeful.
Peaceful, belonging, cherished.

These words are ribbons I tie
around the trunk of a greater tree,

one that wears clouds for canopy,
and disappears into everywhere.

And Everything.

Beautiful Soul.
You bless my heart and being
with your angelic words.

I am eternally grateful for the gift
of your Love.

For the way you see me.

Your words and sentiment wash over me,
through me, and make me whole. Heal me.

I cherish the soul you were made to be.
I Love You Deeply.

You are so honoring of who I am.

I have no greater Joy than in your soul
remembering itself.

I thank God to have been found
in being lost in you.

I hold your body close,
as a bud holds its blossom.

I hold your soul closer.
As a bud holds its budding.

I am surrendered.
My resistance passport revoked.

I am dissolved.
Tides have taken my sand.

I have been re-deposited.
Now, I am the shifting of your dunes.
Your yearning is my own.

Your words open me,
perfume that parts my petals.

You are a miracle bird
who has settled in my canopy,

and made my forest cry
with your birdsong.

I take your whole being into my heart,
which was created for Infinite Love,
so that I may Love you Infinitely.

Every tremor and rustling
of your priceless soul.

I Love your soul.
I Love your soul.
I Love your soul.

Holy Soul.

I Love your Grace.
The God Beauty in you.

I Love your voice, your laughter,
your intelligence, softness, tenderness,
thoughtfulness, caring, seeing...

your decency, sincerity, depth,

your Light, your Love.

I pray for you
in the fiber of my moments.
May God Bless your Sacred Soul.

Grace protect your body and being
today as you travel these moments of day.

May your gifted soul bless many lives
through the servitude for which you travel.

You are my mystic fountain, the water
where I drop my coins of tears.

I am in Love with you.
Inside of Love.

With you.

My soul wants this intimacy with you.

Ever so close, your breath my breath,
your scent my scent,

one continuous tender kiss,
Forever.

Amor...
No puedo vivir sin ti.

Eres me aire. Mi cuerpo.
Mis sueños. Mi todo.

Love...
I cannot live without you.

You are my air. My body.
My dreams. My everything.

You are my sun,
my solar culture.

I am a spare turtle
adrift from a distracted tribe.

I have come to your rock to bask
and warm my innerness.

I need you next to me,
warming my soul.

In the quietude, Love's ribboning dance,
sweet breath merged,

the world fallen away...
and You.

You have parted my deepest waters with
your unfathomable profundity of soul,

with your phenomenal language.

You have me so in Love with you.
I am undone. Unraveled. Ruined.
Rebuilt.

I am a pyramid in the jungle,
possessing endless passageways
that lead to a center stone.

At night, starlight shines
through my highest apogee,
its beam reaching down to the stone.

Then, you speak.

A brighter light yet
shoots up from my center,

a fissure whose lips
release your Light to a black sky
that no longer sleeps.

Make my past and future deciduous.
Kiss me.

You breathe your words on me,
and I disintegrate into a pool
of Love-struck tears.

I am stunned. Your language
fits precisely into the empty spaces
of my Amazonian desire.

Your aura binds up the world-frayed
fibers of my essence.

Your longing is the synchronicity
to my pronounced yearning.

The more you pour,
the more I remember you
from before this world.

You are why I have never been satisfied
with another.

Because I was remembering you.

And as you remember
your own soul,

you unearth the artifacts
of my Truest Love.

I am a star in the night sky,
pawning my astral position,

so that I may fall into your orbit
and dissipate in your light.

I am moon, my skin flushed and bright,
taken with your sunlight.

You have peeled my outer layers
and found my virginal center,
never before breached by humankind.

What you have always been,
is a Holiness whose scent
I have forever tracked.

You are the jasmine I dream of
for my sacred garden.

The fountain whose water
feeds my every flower.

This is not a poem.

It is my soul saying,
All that I am and ever was
belongs inside of you.

Last night,
you wrote a poem on my bare back
with the pen of your finger,
in the ink of almond oil.

I could not see what you were writing,
but I could feel your heart petition
burn its language into me.

When God created my soul
and its yearning,
your soul and song were so conceived,
to fulfill and complete my persona.

I desire only your language
wrapped around me, a Native blanket,
for the rest of my life.

I wish to drink only your expression
to soothe my thirst the rest of my days.

I pray to bathe in the sunlight
of only your alphabet
for my remaining summer on earth.

Please, stay close to me,
whisper your sweet patois
into my ears as I wake,

as I drift to sleep.

Visit me in my dreams,
speaking your dreamy dialect.

Inhabit my heart forever,
singing your mystical,
miraculous semantic
that carries me to my primal river
and dips me down,

baptizing my soul
in the Holy Intentions
of my Creator.

A Godly meadow has been spread out
by those Awesome Hands.

I wish only, with you, to live and die here,
an indescribable, warm, union breeze
washing over our ecstasy,

while we lie entangled,
our hearts throbbing,
humming a singular song of Love.

I receive your bounty.
And unto you I grant
my entire acreage of existence.

Unto you.

It is a new day.

I am sitting on the large roots of
a pine tree, growing on an overhang
above a river.

A canopy of pine branches are my roof
beneath the roof of sky.

And I am with you,
in the sound of clear current running
over polished stones,

rapids slowing in alcoves of shallows,
pooling by the banks,
brilliant in the early light.

River language is beautiful.
Birds are singing.

I am so greatly blessed and Loved.
By God, the Great Spirit.
And by you.

What a cathedral of pine,
what a sanctuary riverside
in which I am to become a vessel.

These holy grounds of nature
are the splendor I want with you.

What we have is a gem.
A rare dream that others
can only vaguely remember at dawn,

that we are to live and cherish
for the rest of our days.

You are a treasure chest
that I ask with such gratitude
to open for me.

Bless you for opening.

Love's personality is not closed.
It is open.

Love is the spirit of life.
Its sole act is to open.

And the sole responsibility
of all living things,
is to be Love's brigade,
and open.

For Love must be generated continuously.
With infinite appetite.

It is in the Grand design.

Love must be made.
Love must be made.
Love must be made.

A flower makes Love.
Sky makes Love.
Clouds. Grass. Rocks.

Lightning. Thunder. Silence.

An acorn opens its heart to sun
before it becomes an oak.

Hydrogen and oxygen
make Love so naturally.

Life on earth drinks and survives
on the miracle that comes from that.

Sun makes Love boldly.
Moon, like a candle.
Water, with such Grace.

Now, here we are, you and I.
We must do our part.

We have a bond.
It must be meant to help end
some global drought.

Our bodies are only
the drum major in this act.

We have one commandment:
To make Love.

To open, soul and spirit.
Heart and mind.

This is not such a given.

For the world of human flowers
is burdened with an eternal frost of fear.

Fear is a closer.

And so, against the dust of fright,
and the bellows of insecurity,

still, we yawn, wide and tremendous,
breaching all sheaths and layers,

broaching the intense awakening
and flush of nakedness.

Still, you and I, we open.

We make this Love,
and fill our Holy quota.

Come, make this Love with me.

I must confess this revolution
overtaking my soul.

In my mind, I have met you in the secret
garden for a million nights of passion.

Always, we end as clouds lifting toward a
bright moon, lanterns lifting, a quietude
embracing us entirely.

Over and over, this Pouring.

This River spectacular and pure.
This Grand Canyon of dreaming.

The endless Creation in whose presence
I am humbled to dust.

Nothing stirring inside my cavern
but a sublime song of you.

Mi corazon esta contigo.

Por siempre.

Te Amo, Preciosa.
Te Amo.

Ya'at'eeh.
It is good.

The Grace of patience
descends upon us.

My heart is a swallow,
curious and wandering,

swallowed by the bright cave
of your aura.

I am inside your soul.

All night I called out your name.
I was feeling you so deeply.

All day I have been consumed in you.

Aching to hear your voice, to be near you.
I too am crying your name.

You resurrect my entire being.

I have died, to be born again
as your favorite flower.

I will die again,
if it lets me grow once more

inside the soul of you.

Sunrise,
you have been dishonored,
assaulted and abandoned.

I have found your mineshaft
in the woods, overgrown
with what time does with neglect.

Calmaté, Amor.
I have come with my machete.
The clearing away has already begun.

Your own first strokes
are what caught my attention.

Now, together, we build this sanctuary
of honor, this shelter for your repose.

So many days, you have wept
private tears, grooving your terrain
with arroyos and erosion.

Now, restoration has commenced.
We will rebuild this ground.

Grain by grain...
healing, growing.

I start by listening.
Deeply.

With heart dilated.
Soul perforated.

Listening to the sound
of your life journey,
the patter of its rain,

and the way your sunlight
cracks open seeds of beauty
scattered along the way.

Hózhó.

Let's walk this
Way of Balance and Beauty.

Let us Sand Paint this Love.

I am remembering the high plateau
where we first met.

The astounding silence there,
so far away from human stirrings.

The pounding silence,
air so full of Grace.

I rounded a bend, breathless, spent.

You reached the mountain pass,
your eyes watery, weary, wishing.

What had already been joined,
was brought together now in flesh.

Recognition was instantaneous.
Synchronicity commenced.

A harmony like April.

You shook so beautifully,
a leaf in God's purposeful wind.

The sacred wellspring of my heart
and soul leapt up at your nearness,
my emotion waters stirring powerfully.

You are a Divining stick,
summoning my soul water
from depths untouched.

My sand parts before your precious breath.

The river I truly am comes forth,
drawn by Love,

drawn by a preordained season,
arrived and blessed.

I am a bamboo reed who bends
to your aura and song.

I lean into your warm heart light,
wanting your Love to saturate me.

Please, dance your joy and delight
on this earth I am.

Dance your bare feet and nakedness
inside my amorous chambers.

Dance your beauty into a glistening wonder,
that I may cry at your uncontainable glory.

Let me flood my soul and then your own
with the dissolution of my self-binding,

with an unrepentant jailbreak into Love's
unhinging prairie.

I have fallen apart completely,

the only way God allows me
to fall into your Love entirely,

and be transformed into vapor
whose only residence

is the center of the mystic sun
I know your soul to be.

Undone.

Speechless.

My soul completely alive.

Up now in candlelight and music,
poetry pouring through me as I let the
words have their way.

You did this to me.
I cannot sleep. I am on fire.

I am the moisture on your sweet skin.
The warmth of your breath.
The lush affection of your valley.

I am the bird on a branch watching
over you. The night owl sounding,
orienting your dreams to serenity.

The tincture to soften your life callouses.
The ointment to fade your scars and
blemishes.

I am the weeping inside your weeping.
The ache inside your yearning.

You are fire.
I am your burning.

Calmaté, Querida.
Estoy contigo.

Daydreaming of desire.

My hand on your belly,
a broad palm leaf
upon your tenderness.

Picking produce straight
from the wild field.

Feeling for that perfect ripeness,

feeling breeze running
over skin, through fingers,

pulling what is finished and ready
from its soft bed.

You and I have both died away
from this world, my Love,

and been born into
Love's consuming union.

What has been fused by Grace
may not exist except in the exclusive
Love dream of one another.

Show me the way
to the treasury of your desire.

I will polish every single coin.

The paradise within you
has a greater paradise within it.

I am an earnest homesteader.
Permit me to farm that Holy land.

We are a Wind Horse,
wearing the skin of a water bug.

Time to break free
from that restrictive clothing,
and assume our true dimension.

We are an owl.
We feast on night.

During day,
we swim ribbons of light.

Then we climb from those rivers,
lie on hot white sand shores,

and dry our hard breathing bodies
in the blessing breeze.

You say that I undo you.

In my undoing,
I am also undone.

You have a way of feeling me, deeply.

When you do, I am already there,
in the deep of you, feeling.

The eager desire in a hummingbird
for its primal meal of nectar,

is my desire for your sweet spiraling
mist, your fields of sugarcane.

What a bee wants from flower's pollen,
I want from the flower of your tenderness.

Wolves howling at a burning moon
feel the same burning

that incinerates my composure
as I yearn for you.

I once was a lake,
content with its plentiful water.

Now I want the infinite ocean
that is my Love for you.

Blessed Morning, Beloved Angel.

Your sweet breath and pulse
are what move me dreamily
into Sacred day.

I am caught in the delirious
mouth of inspiration,

a prey bird who forever stalks me
from the high branches.

I am about to ask its release,
so I may sleep and renew.

Then I will awaken early
and be swept away again,
to meet you at the nesting place.

May Glory and souls be served.

I will be awaiting your arrival.
That I may know my Love
is safe and dreaming.

That I may therefore drift and dream.

You are the Love fire that warms me,
the manna that feeds me,
the spirit that fills me.

The Light that carries me away.

May Holiness lift us serenely
into Love's atmosphere today.

Usurp my throne.

Send your legions
into my private chambers.

Have them tear up the bedding
and hold me down against the cool,
naked floor.

I will repent,
confess all of my heart's
truant wanderings.

Replace my candles
with your impossible brilliance.

Light up the dingy corners
of this now shocked room.

Burn away the webs and shadows.

Sweep your brightness over this
stale dusk dimness.

Freshen the weeping
I do as a daily chore.

Bid your archers
release a thousand arrows
over my castle walls.

Eclipse the sun with your assault.
Darken sky. Reap moon's memory.

Blister my moat with your passion fire.

I abdicate what power I held.
It is yours. Wield it against my remains.

I am a forbidden city. Enter me.
Populate my court with your natural scent.

Don't wash.

Mark this territory that is my life
with the spices Love's pestle grinds
inside your tender mortar.

Send those snowy messenger doves aloft
with notes writ in blood and mist.

Send them flocking to the roof of existence.

Let them perch among the angels,
and leave word of this mundane unraveling.

I am no king, and you are no queen.

I am an illiterate scribe babbling
by a secret brook.

You are the language of paradise,
flowing through an unknown cavern.

I look into your spring water
for my articulation.

You are the crystal sayings
that rise like silver effervescence
through the pristine ebb and gurgle,

to pronounce my surrender
in miraculous tongue.

I wade in shallow waters looking
for coins of shells,

to string you a necklace
fit for Divinity.

You are the strong breeze
over the deeper bay,
pinnacling as you reach me,

turning me in your breakers,
smashing me to gypsum grain,

a fine silt of awe so small and particulate,

I fit easily through the fissure
leading inward to your virgin cove.

I repeat a mantra that begins with YOU.

You interrupt gently, and offer an older
script that ends with BEGIN.

June's lost flowers are rediscovered in your
eyes of meadow and petals,

blowing their billowing seed
out into galloping gusts of seduction

that drift like wisps of silk in the direction
where I have buried solitude.

Nocturnal creatures,
purring and stalking,

curve their fluid forms
around sedentary trees,

ever closer to the structure that houses day,
ever proximal to sunrise's first notes,

that reading room where Love's letters
are littered along the windowsill,
and rampant around the floor,

pieces of a vision settled in the

grooves of a hardwood luster,

embedded in comfort pillows
that catch like cashmere your sleepiness,

and draw you down to an after-passion
sleep, your skin still wet and cooling.

I wait there in that encampment,

my fingers roughened by pitch
and kindling prior to the fire.

Now you are a sleeping sonnet
woven into my air.

I see your spirit in the space
between the flames,

dancing a fluid grace that charms
my tears again,

sending them over the cusp
of my heart barrel,

seeping through my pores and planks,

perspiring my wood now aged with a
timeless soaking in wine of yearning,
grapes of longing, wrath of burning,

insidious creeping of vineyard tendrils
through my trellis,

through my latticework,
where once my roots were situated
securely.

You have overturned the landscape,
disrupted the soil.

My beginnings are upside down
and staring at a featureless sky,

dazzled by a hypnotizing blue.

I am the redwood laid down, retired,
humming as my fiber churns to dust

in the maws of a million mystic termites
made of glass and glory,

sparked from within by a pulse of light
divinely sourced and flickering
against life's eternity.

You are the sacrament on my tongue.

As I close my mouth,
I feel you melt into my baptismal ecstasy.

You disappear into the dream my soul bore
eons before notions of romance sprung like
roses from the soil of human instinct.

You are the pews, stained wonderfully.

I am the cracks in between,
pining for your attention,

aging with you as you age,
oiling your length and breadth
and depth in the substance of adoration,

I am the creaking that bears all weight
placed upon your enduring wood.

I am the draft
through the cracked open window,

and the uprising of colors on light beams
through stained glass that portrays your
aura, and epic journey.

I walked a dust storm,
hoping at best for a pause in the blindness.

Then came you, and sky opened its clarity,

offered a deep well amidst the nothingness
with water so sweet and clean,
I thought it tears of angels.

Then came you,
and the purifying rain announced
with a scent of air so intoxicating,

and the first stalks of green
with buds of promise,

and sound of water falling,
and stone music at the bottom
of a clear lagoon.

And then came you,
oasis filled with fruit and shade,

and ribbons of poetry splashed
on canvases of leaves,

and silence flowering,
and a wisp of sensuality growing
from a grove of willow song.

I entered Love's chapel,
and there you were,

minister, congregation,
rafters, reverent air.

I sat at your ivory statue,
witnessed your tears running
toward the floor.

I caught them in my palms and drank,
a potion that carried me
into a further sanctuary,

and there you were,
scripture, floating and diaphanous.

You entered my membrane
and reordered my composition.

What I was,
was no longer what I was.

Once, I was corn stalk
in an abandoned field.

Now I was corn pollen
in a ceremony of dancers and drummers,
and holiness that cannot be pantomimed.

I entered Love's chapel,
and there you were,

the prayer I had always uttered.
The praise I had deeply offered.

The worship my breath bequeathed.

I entered Love.
You were its chapel.

I entered your chapel.
Love entered me.

I died into a birth
unprecedented and unrecordable.

I became the *Ahhh* in the breast of men.

I became *Amen*.

Eternity.

I will plant a cherry seed
and endure the seasons of its growth
into a fruit bearing tree,

just so I can taste
the day and moment

of placing that single cherry
on your blushed lips,
on your hospitable tongue.

All so that I can behold
your succulence
embracing that succulence,

its ripe, engorged
concentration of years
disappearing into your mouth of desire.

All so that I may witness
the dark juice run
to the corners of your mouth
of sensuality

and stream down your chin,
over your delicate tundra.

That I may drink from that stream
with my lips sculpted to lift moisture
from your body,

lips suffused with fullness
to touch your skin
as sky touches meadow,

softness against softness
until your softness gives way to ecstasy
and evaporates into Light.

From seed to tree to fruit to paradise
in a moment like this.

I will wait like this,
patience a cloud I ride willingly.

Until the spectral climax.

Until the rainbow that makes
all rainbows appear as dust in sky.

I will wait for such a moment as this,
to feed your lips of air
the deep red cherry,

the achingly ready fruit,
of my Divini-Tree.

What is this glacial melting?

My canyons are overtaken.
Spring's runoff is so pure and gushing.

I am Diné fry bread,
baking in the clay oven of Union.

I am sweat on the skin of a delirious
soul in a dark sweat lodge song.

You see me below you,
at the foot of a high seaside cliff.

All around are rocks,

but I am romance,
and I am calling out:

Plunge, Love,
and I will catch you.

I have delayed the tides
and softened the sand
with tears of blatant gratitude.

What we are growing is not fantasy.
It is ministry.

We have been served unto
each other, that our Evidence
may be served unto the world.

Plunge, my Angelic Ark.

I am in this profound Love
with you.

Dear, Precious Gemstone.

I cannot believe the poetry
that pours from your spring.

You make Rumi's words
dust in my mouth

as I swallow your poetic
amber and honey.

If you would please,
speak these Grace-soaked words
into my heart and soul forever.

I will be finished with yearning.

Your soul language,
your spirit tongue,

is the most beautiful
I have ever known.

And your voice.
Your voice is a song
I can sleep to, endlessly.

The perfect pitch and tone
to sooth my being.

Together, your word and sound
dissolve me, condense my tears
like water on the surface of my soul.

Blessed Light of Compassion,

Please do not despair,
for this Love should grant you Peace.

Our togetherness is as assured
as the rings of growth
intimately bound
in the fiber of ancient trees.

You fill my moat with mystic Love
and set it gladly afire.

My castle crumbles.

I am left nothing more than
a naked beggar who wants only
to be consumed in nakedness.

Beg with me among the Aspen trees.
Wind will carve our humility.

Leaves will fall, yellow and auburn,
from the branches of time.

And we will spark a fire
in the whispering woods around us.

Our burning will join us
with the old growth.

One day, something new.

Even before what we are now,
you were moon,

pulling at the emotional tide
of my syncopated soul.

I want deep inside your earth.

Let me pick out your stones
and soften your soil.

I want to work your clay
in my hands and sweet water.

I want inside your sun.

Once sun, I want inside your sky.

Once sky, finally, host me
in your borderless universe.

Wrap your roots around me.

Make them my cloak and robe.

Let me drink from the nectar
that drips from your flower.

Permit me to inhale the primal scent
from the nooks of your branches.

I want inside your soul,
where I may seep through your cavern,

and you may weep me out onto the soft
meadow of your face, in Love,

only to draw me back
inside your sensitivity.

I want inside your earth.

Moon is our Mecca.
We walk into that bright cascade,

shedding clothes and scars,
sloughing old skin and sensibilities.

Who wants the soberness of rules,
when Freedom is in town?

You and I, we recognize no
common keepers of the law.

Our jail has already been dynamited.

The wanted posters are flying
in the wind.

I have always wanted to be on the run.

The stories you tell with your eyes,
make this great escape worth all hardship.

Even as we make camp and fire
in the thick brush outside of town,

I cannot wait to hold you
as we sleep.

You against me
is my favorite part of day.

And perhaps our innate alignment.

Sunrise is our Jerusalem.

Waking takes me from wishful dreams
in which our solitude spreads its dowry
over all living things.

We become the breath of Harmony,
pulsing through Creation,
a wind in perfect pitch.

There are times when,
if we are being honest,
we must admit that we travel
with wolves,

sometimes going our own way,
sometimes laughing at the pack.

Always caring to bless the den
with the visions we have seen,
looking through our secret window.

True Lovers forever ache
for the high mountain pastures,
where they can refine their union.

Crowds gathered for no reason
but boredom and insecurity
offer such breed no attraction.

Nor does gossip turn their ears.
Great Silence already has them occupied.

When the sun goes down,
let's you and I come up,

into the brilliance and stirring
of sacred talking, which has no words.

Just flashes of light in the eyes
that translate the passion of soul.

And raindrops on the lip
that moisten the meadow
where we meet and fall.

The basket weavers are all saying
you are their favorite customer
at the market.

You come daily with crates full
of fresh picked lemons, plums,
and avocados.

And leave with the weavers'
newest crafts.

I am reminded of the way
you come for my affection,

and leave with the sweetest happiness
written on your face.

Somehow, each time we meet like this,
I end up covered in the fragrance
of an entire orchard,

and feeling as though
I have just gorged on all its fruit.

One wild night,
you took me on a global adventure,
just by the way you moved against me.

I will always remember
the scent of the places,
the feel of those memories:

Rickshaw. Gondola.
Banjul. Accra.

Kigali. Zamfara.
Bamako. Juba.

Khartoum.
Addis Abbaba.

We don't need grand moments
to feel the bursting of our joy.

A current can run inside a teapot,
just as it can in the ocean.

Just brush my shoulder as you walk by.
Hold your glance for an extra beat.

If I touch even your thigh or neck,
I feel the pleasure of your deeper gardens.

As long as we slow down enough
inside life's seductive cyclone
to hear birds land on branches,
to feel branches push out their buds,

then we are in the stillness that allows
us to hear our mutual heartbeats,
and respond to them,
sucklings to our milk.

All continents have their pain and glory.

Be my continent.

We will drift,
conjoined and tectonic.
Our geology unrepentant.
Nomadic as we bare our roots.

Your sweetness seals all the cracks
and fissures of my years.

Melts all my glaciers
into freshwater lakes,
where I bathe in this revival.

I need you to know how fierce
my fire is for you.

My embers have a passionate calling:

to volcanically reshape your earth
in the image of this Holy Love,
this Sacred Yearning.

Your sweet soul is the music
to which my notes belong.

You are the thousand candles
illuminating my spirit,

flickering against the walls
of my sanctuary,

dancing a movement
of miraculous beckoning,

drawing me into your heat,
where I burn away what I was
and become what I am:

element of this union,
filament of your burning,

and ever more delirious in Love.

⁓

Will you please come sleep with me?

Your incredible, mystic words
only make me desperate

to feel you against me,
me against you.

Your language is the only library
I wish to plunder.

Burn all the rest.

I want to follow the trail of your words
back to your lips, your tongue, your throat,

your chest, your heart,
the flower that is your soul.

I want to nest there in the petals
that cup your sweetness.

I want to pull your tenderness
over me, a dreamy blanket,

and sleep without end in this bliss
of your scent and shadow,

your pools and streams that sing
and weep such Glory,

your earth that drums my spirit in
irresistible treble.

I want you now and completely.

Spend this whole night
inside the warm cloak of my arms.

I know you have been restless.

I promise to be a sedative
with no side effect.

Except dreams with no end
that taste like something
braised by sugar and sun.

You are a faithful fountain.
Your pouring astounds my soul.

It evaporates my heart's walls,
sweeps me into the core
of Love's fateful flame.

I am restless.

When everyone is asleep,
meet me in the garden.

Let's eat cake at midnight.

We'll stoke the fireplace,
then show it how to burn.

In the morning,
I'll feed you sopaipillas,

or dutch babies,
or strawberries and cream.

I am a hive of bees.
Consumed with making Love.

It is best that others don't bother me.

When I am in this mood,
I cannot moderate my instincts.

I either make honey,
or I swarm what gets in the way
of making honey.

My appetite for this sweetness
cannot be tamed.

My DNA has been switched on.
I am genetically inflamed.

Blessed Morning, Dear Flower.

I pray you are Peaceful
inside your heart.

You know that your presence
parts me like the Red Sea.

All my enslaved woundedness
crosses over into Love's Paradise.

I once was an eagle,
perched on a tall tree,
watching you walk the Trail of Tears.

I would have done anything
to keep you from such suffering.

I gave away all my sacred feathers,
so that I could take this human form.

But I am still flying,
and I still watch you walk
your many tender trails.

If you look up and see me swooping,
know that I dive to consummate
this voracious burning,

to let what is flesh in us turn to ash,
to vapor, to Sky's eternity.

I want to swallow you
entirely into my heart,

birth you out into your
own Divine freedom,
through the ether
of our ecstatic union.

I want you like wholeness
wants its Holy completion.

Let me paint your lips
in the rouge of my passion.

Let me moisturize your skin
in my essential oils,

polishing you as a river stone,
over long and faithful seasons,

washing over you in tears
and sweet water,

cradling your delicate heart leaves
in my strong and sturdy branches,

swaddling you in my garden
of inner Peace,

feeding you breakfast
beneath the canopy,
beside the black bamboo,

making deep, long Love with you,
sweet as jasmine after April rain.

Let me make your rose blush like this,
over and over, recklessly...

Wreck this sea,
this bed of normalcy.

Let's pull this blanket of passion
over our burning bodies,

and disappear from this world
in unfathomable rapture.

Let us kiss each other
into a legendary epiphany of bliss.

Let's Love like this.

Moon's ethereal face is pocked
by the kisses of eons of asteroids.

The face of my soul is pocked forever
with the beauty marks

of your Love storm against my surface,
down into my throes,

where my roots sip buried spring water
and moan their delight.

You have marked my soul's face forever
with your luscious eyelashes of affection,

with their batting and sweeping
across my unshaded ground,

with your gaze that sets fire
to my dry prairie,

with the colorful gondola
of your life journey
that has brought you over oceans

and down serpentine canals
to reach my cay,

with your conch and shell
that you bring from the tide

to deflower and grill with me
on hot beach stones,

so that we may dine upon sand,
beside water's rhythmic massage,

under a profound black sky
and all its brilliant cosmic jewelry,

to gaze uninterrupted
at that Sistine chapel,

to fall asleep so sweetly,
bodies enmeshed,

on a blanket,
covered in night's warm breeze,

dreaming of our union,
even as we sleep unified and sealed,

waking to a considerate sun
that slowly teases our dozing,

slowly rousing our bodily embers
so cued for desire,

making Love on a blanket
of sand's softness,

sunrise coating our skin in Light
as we Love,

wet and gasping in the aftermath,
bathing in sea's swollen splendor,

joining again in the water,
our fevered bodies surging with the tide,

feeding your lips a fresh breakfast
of mango and pineapple,
and milk of coconut,

washing you in my gaze of Love,
cooling you gently in my breath,

carrying you in my arms
back into ocean,

where we slip warmly
into the deep of life,

beneath the sea and its vivid coral
choreography of life and species,

where we deliriously dissolve
inside the surrendered faith

and submitted effervescence
of this Love.

Woodpecker wants what lives fat and
promising inside the tree.

I want what lives so swollen and ready
inside your heart.

I will not harm your tree,
for I can only drink from what it offers,

can only swim in its shade
and climb its heights.

Your canopy is my dance floor and skylight.
Your roots, my kindred foundation.

Your branches,
a Love letter to my yearning.

Your willowy leaves,
the tenderness you bequeath
to my delicate heart.

May I please lie down at your feet
and roll over your caring moss?

May I place my lips upon your bark
and stay there until it turns to cotton,
or silk or sunlight?

I want only your softness,
the quilting God spun
prior to our conception.

I am done with hard things.
I pray you will be my meadow,

that together we will be
a meadow for each other, and for this
bruised and battered world.

Seeds have been planted
in this early morning hour.

Now we crack and grow.

Your soul comes up through your face
like a dolphin surfaces from the deep.

What I see makes me ache
to dive back down with you.

I want to spend my life
gazing upon your face,

the way a mountain gazes for ages
upon sky.

I join you in this vast humility,
this gratitude, and surrender.

I am living an unprecedented Love.

Your soul and life,
inside my life and purpose,
is miraculous for me.

You are Sacred to me.
As is our Love.

In Faith and Peace,
may we walk and breathe in it.

This wildfire is mutual,
and you are an accomplice!

I am the drum your Love plays.
The dance your Desire performs.

My lips have no right being anywhere
but on your acres,
upon your soft lands
and tender territories,

within your fine crevasses
and plush nooks, so privately.

May I plunder your minerals
and make them mine?

I will give them back to you a million fold
in sweet rain and purified showers.

I will be the waterfall
for your lagoon of tranquility.

I will bathe you romantically, sacredly,
passionately, endlessly.

I am your water, your wetness,
your warmth, your welcome home.

It has been raining and storming
since morning.

Let's read books in bed all day,
our legs wrapped like mangrove roots,

our bodies turning the burning
pages of our burgeoning desire.

Love has announced Its arrival
to my pasture.

Wildflowers grow all over the place.
No restraint. Just Happiness run amok.

And a fragrance I cannot say.

I profess such surrender to your
Holy journey of life.

You are walking a rite of passage.
I choose to be a caretaker along the route.

I require no conditions.
Just let me tend the weeds and stones
along with you.

When it rains,
I will scout the woods
to bring you kindling
and ignite your Joy.

What a thing,
to be supernaturally mated.

All that I am has dissolved
into a devotion to serve your soul.

For just as you believe
that I am your assignment,

I see more every day
that you are my assignment,
so clearly and completely Ordained.

To this assignment I say,
Amen. Ashé. Namasté.

Blessed Morning,
my treasured Mate of this Love.

I proclaim that your sweet soul
has absconded with my heart.

No trace is left. No clue or evidence.

You have taken it, and clearly
are doing with it what you please.

Thank Goodness.
I want no retrievals.

Only that you pour your Love
into its cavern, until it becomes
your own blissful beating.

Palpitate my existence
with a persistent fervency
of tidal Love unleashed.

Call back the hounds.
I went AWOL long ago.

I have bid my speechless heart Adieu.

Once, my water was solid.

Your Love touched me,
and my solidity ran wild.

Instantly, I was a crystal lake.

Your lips touched me,
and my lake became mist.

Your breath touched me.
My mist evaporated entirely.

Now I am formless, unseen,
without boundary.

Completely uncontained
and spilling everywhere.

I am the dazed and surrendered wind.

I say Amen, my Sacred Love.

I say Amen.

My Beloved flame of life and beauty.

I am enraptured in the same
fire of wanting as are you.

I am tumbling with you
in a space beyond time,

in a dimension mystic and immaterial,
laced with lavender and honeysuckle.

Where we are is a water drop
inside of sunlight,

and the instantaneous nature
of light itself.

We are the passion of planets,
and the knowing silence of space.

We are what the jungle does to itself
with its infinite vines
and miasmic rebirths.

We are the diaphanous tension
of a raindrop,

and the erotic release of clouds.

When our lips touch,
so do the continents of our Love,

drifting into one another until
your east coast becomes my west coast,

and mountains rise from our valleys,
becoming our peaking desire,

and the unbridled force of our intimacy.

Holy Ground of mine.

Your presence completely annihilates
my composure and constitution.

Nothing of me remains on earth
but this Love. This fire.

I must have you.
I must have you have me.

My sanctity.
My sanctuary.
My soul.

Beloved Prayer and Poetry of mine.

I Love you, my Oasis.
My garden. My dream. My life.

I have dreamt of flowers.
You are the flower of my dreams.

I have yearned for Peace.
You are entry to the Peace of my life.

I have awed to beauty.
You are the most profound Beauty
I have ever beheld.

I have prayed for a Love that feels
so right and harmonious.

You are the righteous harmony
my Love has waited for.

You are my epiphany. My entirety.

My Eternity.

My Sacred Mate.

I vow, now and forever,
to wash your soul
in the Love of God within me.
In the Love that I am.

I vow to tend your garden faithfully.
To give myself to you exclusively.

I vow to cherish and treasure
your every word, every breath,

every hope and desire.

I vow to laugh and sing
and dance with you.

Because these are your passions.
And your passions are the bridge
from my bank over to your shore.

I vow to escape this world with you,
and fall forever into this Love.

I vow to bathe you in my inspired tears,
soak you in my passion water.

To be medicine for your healing,
a safe space for your security,
an arrival for your dreams.

I vow to walk with you,
adventure with you,
discover with you.

To speak, touch, listen, act, and think
tenderly, gently, kindly with you.

I vow to make sweet Love with you,
with all my possible heart and soul.

I vow to kiss you as continuously as rain
falls in a rainforest in its rain season,

as pervasively as sun shines in the desert.
As deeply as oceans dream of being deeper.

I vow to pray with you, submit with you,
obey with you, surrender with you.

To live inside of Holy Love
and Compassion with you.

I vow to be your Love,
your Light, your Life.

My Entire Love.

Bless your sweet heart
and glorious soul this morning.

I have no words for how your
poetry of Love last night
affected me.

God's lips parted.
Your expression came out,

a surreal butterfly.
A perfect angel.

I cannot believe what pours
from your fountain.

And yet your words and sentiment
are exactly the petition

I have sent upward and outward
since before my conception.

I don't want to write words for this,
what you did to me last night.

I am filled with silence.

And the song of a God who has
left me quivering in the bowstring
of Love's Divine arrow.

Quivering along feathers strung
in the harp that exudes a music
only angels may hear.

I am done.

Your words vanish me into Love's
unexplainable dimension.

I am done. And yours.

Redundantly.

94

I ask permission
to mount the stallion of my desire

and ride the prairie length,
from one corner of your lips to the other,

galloping my heartbeat,
my yearning on the reins,

as my lips sigh and sink back and again
against your soft beds and riverbanks.

Only after the risen sun has courted sky
and passed back beneath the horizon,

only when my stallion is spent,

let me tenderly graze your finer pastures
in the lazy light of dusk.

Then to lay down my form,
and beneath night's blanket,

sleep in the rise and fall
of your dreaming breeze.

And when the stars instigate
an earthly revival

in their alignment
deep in the darkness,

let my arroyos fill once more
with mountain flood.

Let me rise then
and move in moonlight
across your prairie once more.

Harness the sun.
Let it be our ring of matrimony.

What burning it does shall be
a microcosm of our burning,

its heat a glimpse of our temperature.

However the expanse
of universal space,

its entirety may fit inside our passion
as a flower bud fits inside the forest.

Our Love is not enormous.
It is the sunburst of Enormity.

We are not charting a course
for mundane Love,

for even from the mundane
we excavate Divinity.

Our very lips are sails
that when bound in bliss,
carry us to Holiness.

Our every wedded moment
has a destiny:

the sanctuary of Miracle
inside our hearts.

And the Chalice of preciousness
composed of our Mated soul.

Oh yes, oh yes, my Love.
I will have you.

In the Love of God,
I will have you.

I take you, now and forever,
as my Holy wife.

My Miracle of Love.

They cannot say this Love,
for its infinity steals the colors
of all who move to paint it.

I thought I had reached the pinnacle
of this life.

Then Love waved at my poor exhaustion
from the true mountaintop, saying,

You are almost there!
Just keep climbing.

Beneath a Japanese maple, with you.

Our bodies, like summer's warm
breeze, stirring.

Our hearts, like maple seeds, falling.

In Love, expanding,
like Day's steady temperature.

Heartbeats syncopated,
like the thrumming of swallows,
mated for life.

Like the twin cadence of turtles,
married, wedded in the shallows,
merged in the deep.

You and I in stillness, like the maple,
a Peace posture allowing God to reign
within us, magnifying our Love radiance.

You and I sheltered, beneath the maple,
in the shade of tenderness.

You and I on a blanket of earth,
tall grass waving,

as we make Love that blesses the maple,
and opens earth's flower.

Creation, beholding our nectar converging,
cries and sings.

I, a soul,
take thee as my Wife.

Beloved Song of my heart.

My Garden.

I am so consumed in you,
my chosen Wife.

God's doing is our undoing.

We are an ancient yarn
unraveling helplessly.

Our threads are delirious
in this ether, this air.

They have no direction but Love.

No idea or rationale but to mate,
to mate, to mate.

How do I contain this body,
when a sun burns inside?

You touch my kindling.
The whole pile explodes in flames.

I am a walking wildfire,
a danger to the world's docility.

Do not look at me.
I will burn down cities at your glance.

If you touch me slightly,
I will torch nations.

Kiss me,
and continents will be left in ashes.

I am a prayer.
You are the Holy space I run to.

I have orders to scavenge the innards
of your heart and bring what I find
to your lips,

so that you may *say me* out loud,
a mantra of fulfillment.

Say your great desire.
Make manifest my reason for being.

Let me finally materialize,
like moisture on the glass,
like mist in the valley.
Dew on the clover.

I have waited lifetimes
to come into being
inside your being.

Release me from this long potential,
into a serene storm of spirit and union.

Carry me on your skin
as beads of condensation.

Let me pool in your pores,
desert rain after drought.

If, before, you were an arid land,

let me arrive as monsoon
and flood your canyons.

Let the miracle of new life
take hold in these nubile waters.

Carry me on your lips
as a secret plundering
that your every word reveals
to those in the furnace of Love.

Tattoo my heartbeat
on your unseen areas.

Feel this throbbing
inside your sensitivity.

Sew my voice
into the fabric of your being,

so I may whisper with total access:
I Love your soul.

Please, check my credentials.

You will see that I was sent
by Love's Creator to renovate your heart,

and landscape your life
into a feasible fantasy.

I have brought birds and fountains
and fragrant vines. Let us begin.

You and I are a single Bird of Paradise
with a thousand-year sleeping phase.

Now our bloom has come.

It will keep parting like this for eternity,
opening, opening,

spreading our pheromones
like flocks of clouds in spring.

Do not blame me for this outburst.

I was told to pour out
all of my Love, urgently,

into the first clay jar
that looks like it can hold the sky.

I was told that when I found a fountain
that never stops weeping,

that would be the place to place
all my tears.

I heard clearly the Voice that directed:

When I stumble upon a tenderness
that only wants to nurture me,
look deeply into its intent and nature.

If I see my own Love gazing back at me,
I am home.

At that point, I should break all leases
and throw away my old belongings.

For I will never need anything again inside
this Fashioned nakedness of Love.

If I am overboard with this desire,
it is only because I am obeying the Wind
that brought me to your meadow,

and told me to become
your unencumbered wilderness.

I have found your land.
I will obey.

I will never again grow anywhere
but inside this Love.

I am a species of one,
native to your soul and soil.

I cannot be transplanted.

To the world I say,

"Leave me alone to grow here,
where I was intended."

To you, my Love, I say,

take me by the roots
and swallow me whole.

I care only to be inside you,
filling every empty space
you have ever known.

I have such a Lovesickness.

I am crazy and burning.
My chest never stops exploding.

I wake to your Loving words,
and right away again,

the inferno leaps up
to resume its cause.

I don't have words.

My spirit took them last night,
when it left from me and ran to you.

I need to be with you,
my exquisite Wife.

My lips caressing your soft skin
until you moan your pleasure
and wake the lion in me.

You are holding my breath,
which I cannot retrieve
until I am with you again.

Let me shower you in my passion.
Soak you in my rain.

Let me make this Love with you
from this day forward,

as the constant climate
of our matrimony.

I am a bear,
newly roused from a long hibernation,
just emerging into the bright sunlight of
your beauty.

While still deep in my dozing,
I caught the scent of you
the moment you turned your soul
in my direction.

With your first glance,
you lifted me from my repose
like a flower seed in morning's whisper.

You were a soul charmer,
summoning me from my basket of solitude
with the flute music your lips played.

I had never heard your mating call
before among humankind.

And so, I left my winter cave
to approach your mystic serenade
and decipher your unfamiliar code.

Now, exposed and naked in
the brightness of this Love,

I am completely bewildered.
I have lost all emotional bearing.

My heart is no longer an organ.
It has replaced my bones and skin.

I am covered in Love,
structured in Passion.

I have lost my appetite
for indifference.

Give me the burning bush.

Give me the sunset
of your oceanic eyes closing.

Give me the sunrise
of your warm eyes opening.

I want midnight,
and your constellation
spread before me.

And the comet shower
of your wandering touch.

Please me with the spring water,
filtered through your thousand years
of yearning.

Let me sip the pure result.

Have me as your obsessive gardener.
Don't send me home.

No matter how many hours I spend
in the earth bed of your happiness,

I will still have so much
passion work to do.

The rumors are true.

Love has infinite disciples,
and I am its greatest fanatic.

A single word from your lips
is my sermon for a lifetime.

Even your sigh leaves my heart
inscribed with a sacred commandment:

Love this one.

I am a well in the desert
brimming with passion water,
even as I endure this world's aridity.

You are the miraculous source
that fills me.

I am a sea turtle up from the deep.

My shell, a letter opener
carving ocean's envelope

so that I may read the currents
of your Love

and know that I am home.

Your Beauty is like coral reefs
turned into the brightest diamonds,

glistening so brightly that sun squints,
and heaven draws its shades.

You cannot deny the earthquake
at my epicenter that now ripples

your heart like a carpet snapped
in the dewy air of spring.

If you are lightheaded,
it is because I am lighthearted,

levitated in the same matrimonial
yearning that claims your composure.

Love has laid out a blanket
in a meadow shimmering in sunlight
and painted with breeze.

Meet me there.

We will pour the wine of passion
and I will bring to your lips

the finest morsels
dipped in dark Divine chocolate.

And we shall not return.

Let my fingers parade
over your avenues.

Wake to my drumbeat
on your nerve endings.

Wake to my gallantry
upon your hills.

No more distance.
Only tumbling and heat.

Chant my name
as I chant my rhythm
into your valley.

I am a Santa Ana wind.

What I bring, was heated in the desert,
crackles with that intensity.

Undulate with me. Mate with my fire.
I want your fine soft majesty.

Shower in the open nature
of my skies opening and pouring.

Feel my force. Climb my mountain.

Reach the pinnacle and scream your
pleasure all over the slopes.

Open your primal voice.
Let me hear your supernova's arrival.

Descend like a monk
with nowhere else to go,

no hurry, just a long,
tender meditation of touching.

Drink from my pools.
Roll over my moss.

Scale me again.
Over and over, take me.

Make my mountain
your climbing obsession.

Expedition me to exhaustion.

Then, trembling,
with nerve endings dancing,

climb into my arms
for a perfect sleep
only Inspired Lovers may know.

We have so much waking to do.
Our embers can only simmer
so long.

Every sweet particle
and play of this world
is my way of saying
my Love for you.

Look at that fountain
gushing in summer.

That is how I Love you.

And that dove song,
my Love for you.

Sun's penetration of sky.
The slope of a rainbow.

Arrows arching over a castle wall.
Symbiosis of flowers and bees.

Honeysuckle scent.
A stallion nuzzling his mare.

Bucks rutting.
The fourth leaf of a clover.

The virginal opening of a rose.
Rock avalanches. Polar caps melting.

You are the cause of my climate change.

You are the suspect who raided my
contentment and left me with this desire.

All wildfires are but a whisper of this
burning Love I am, for you.

Let's set the forest on fire.

Please come, undress,
and fall onto me, a leaf onto water.

I will take you down into my current,
and you will know my Love for you.

My being churns for you,
a galactic waterwheel
drunk on the very Holy water
into which it plunges.

I am a soul
in the Hand
that made me.

You are the soul I was handed to
at the moment of my making.

Nothing else exists for me,
except through the Glorious prism
and ferocious fire
of my eternal Love for you.

I was a giant redwood.
Your Love cut me down.

I had lived that way long enough.

Now I am something larger,
deeper, freer, truer.

I am sky, sun, soul.

I am a leaf caught in a Gust
that shepherds me
in an exclusive direction:

a Matrimonial, Mated,
forever Loving life with you.

I am helpless.
You are my Helper.

I am surrendered.
Your Love, my Conqueror.

By virtue of Holy Intent,
I bow this soul I am to you.

Holy and Great Spirit,

I make my offering
of cedar and sage.

I spill my soul
on the ground of my life,

in gratitude for You.

How You have blessed my soul.
How You have rendered me mute in awe.

With the Love of this woman,
You have applied the tourniquet

to staunch the bleeding
that was my aloneness.

With one Breath,
You ended my wandering,

and faced me to the Mate
who is my home.

I will never search again.

What Love You give me,
I bequeath to her.

I want no sunset without her gaze.
No sunrise apart from her touch.

You have entrusted me with her most
Divine and Caring heart.

With the Love that I am,

I will build her sanctuary,
and protect the rare artifact
and Supreme gift she is.

We are submerged up to our chests
in the glowing warm tide.

Its movement moves us. We are
water lilies bobbing. Seeped into.

I am holding you, so close.
Your legs wrapped around my waist.
Your face in the nook of my neck.

In moonlight.

No sound but lapping waves,
and heartbeat.

I have arranged for Creation to pause,
for just this moment.

Day is a darkness
next to the way you light my life.

Your past is a bridal veil
I lift from your face.

I propose Eternity.

Please, marry me.

Be my wife.

My heart is more tender than most.
Your kindness is the rare nurse I require.

My needs have been a herd
of long-bleating goats.

Your soul is the sweet grass
for their hunger.

The soft ground for their bedding.
The pristine water for their thirst.

Your beauty, the awesome panorama
that holds their gaze.

If I even catch the scent of Holy scripture,
I know that Word calls me to you.

I have given away all my old belongings.

I need sheer emptiness,
so that I may be filled with you.

I am on my knees in the deep dark soil,
pleading to you:

Please, take me as your Husband.
Have me as your Mate.

I will be your Paradise,
doused in Holiness,
soaked in Sanctity.

Great Spirit has woven
a gleaming and Glorious web

across the great expanse
of my heart and soul.

The web has no purpose,
but to hold you in its taut vibrato.

Please, my Love, marry me.

Marry me, and I will be for you
what I can only be:

The prayer your soul always uttered.

The affection and honor
for which you live.

The Mate for whom you were shaped.

I will listen to your soul language
with the singular devotion you deserve.

I see your true soul,
my dear sweet mist.

God did this to me.
I have no choice.

I have Miraculous eyes for you alone.

I promise you:

I will live inside your heart,
and grow with you a garden there,

and we will live a Love that leaves you
weeping happiness, fulfilled.

Our Love will be your Peace and Harmony.
Beautiful Love of mine, be my Sacred Wife.

Have me as your Husband.
Join me in this matrimony.

We will make this Love,
in every moment.

And every moment will be
utter glowing evidence
of this Love we make.

I say your name a thousand times
with each heartbeat:

My chant. My drumbeat.

My invocation. My prayer.
My bell chime. My miracle.

My song. My dance. My horizon.
My past. My echo. My desire. My fire.

My burning bush. My oasis.
My salvation and secret.

My waterfall.

My fortress and promise.
My fragrance and foundation.

My softness and strength.

My poem and paradise.
My language. My whisper.

My kiss and soaking.
My climax and crying.

My answer and explanation.

My revelation. My epiphany.

Oh, My Great Beauty.

I am vacated.
Only Love remains.

Bury me in your earth.

Let me become the root
of your pleasure and Joy.

Moan with me on the sand
under a stark sky

jeweled in glimmering
distal bodies.

Gasp with me
through a million private mornings.

You take my breath away.

I don't want it back.
I want yours.

I will run it through my soul
and filter it through my Love.

And when I kiss you,

you will feel your own purified desire
climb back into your heart.

Over and over like this,
we will cycle this matrimony.

You are the Astounding Amen
that completes the Prayer and Purpose
of my life.

My Garden.

Love me with your gentle tongue.

I need your affection. Holistically.
Mystically. Mist with me.

Let's merge, and turn our bodies
to water and Light.

On this day,
I wed myself to thee, Beloved.

I open the carriage that is my soul
and bid thee enter.

We will ride together upon a road
no other has known,

and enter a land
none may possibly conceive.

We will be a single flower
growing in a Godly meadow.

And our Love will blossom endlessly.

On this day, Beloved,
I wed myself to thee.

Sweet Fountain Wife.
My spectacular Gift.

Inside of you,
I find my exclusive belonging.

That I may swell my Love
inside your soul,

and you may know that you are home.

My life has been no more
than the digging of a deep well,

by the invisible Hands of Providence,

and the cloaked concentration
of Circumstance.

With each moment, a rain has fallen.

My well has filled with a water
that cannot be repeated.

Its mineral content is suited
for a demographic of one.

Here, I pool it in my hands,
and offer it to you without condition.

Drink of what I am.

Quench forever your long,
sublime thirst.

Pájaro Mio.
You give me bliss.

I write your every word
on the windows of my memory,

and will never wash that glass.

You are a summer growing
in my cells.

Tall, hearty wild grass
waving my worries away.

A genius Curator selected you
for my heart gallery.

Our two lives have been the work
of one single Artist,

a Phenomenon self-commissioned
to create this Love piece.

Now, we know Love's Peace.

No other assurance
has ever been so complete.

Even our moments apart
are gifts sent to craft our togetherness.

A horse rides in from the distance,
with no rider or saddle.

It has been through deserts and forests,
over mountains, across rivers.

It arrives thirsty, hungry, weak.

I think a single thought of you,
and magically, the horse is fed and watered.

You touch me,
and the horse bucks and neighs.

Love blooms for the millionth time
between us since noon,

and suddenly the horse is strong
and vital, racing beneath harvest moon.

I take thee as my Holy Wife,
Appointed by the Most High,

consecrated upon the grounds
of our Sacred Love.

I wed my eternal soul,
as Directed by my Great Spirit God,

to your eternal soul,
as actuated by Grace.

I vow to be a vessel of God's Love for you,

and therefore to pour out the entirety
of my life in you, and for you,

with the Passionate, Devoted,
and Complete Love
I was born to be,
for you.

Dear Sweet, Priceless Heart,

I offer my existence to you,

for your Divine Love to keep
and hold and Glorify.

Before the Sun that made me,
I give myself to you.

May you and I together
make the Sweetest species of Love
this world has ever known,

and surely has never domesticated.

My Beloved Wife.
My Sweet Sunshine.

My Hope and shelter.
Jasmine fragrance.
Glory Dancer.

I wake only because you exist.
I must come to you.

You draw me from my dreams,
usher me into a Greater Dream
the Almighty is having.

You are the cool water I sip
deep in the desert.

The warm breeze
that melts my frozen tundra.

My rainwater. My firelight.
My orchestra of wonder and praise.

My Holy Ground.
My pilgrimage. My temple.

My rite and ritual.

The electrical impulse that beats my heart.
The lightning in my emotional sky.

The dynamite to destroy all my dams.
The biblical flood that washes me clean.

My repentance. My salvation.
My resurrection. My Sacred sound.

My Sinai Word.
My Commandment.

My Assignment on Earth.
My Godly Love.

My Godly Love.

My Love is the mystic meadow
that you as a little girl
wished to die into,
and be born into bliss.

My Love is that meadow.
You have found me again.

And now, you never have to leave.
I am yours. My roots transplanted.

I am so in Love with you.

You have parted my waters,
and let my ancient tribe
through to this land of Grace.

You possess the most beautiful poetry.

My soul wandered this world nightly,
searching for a song.

One night, I stumbled into a burning bush.

On its ash, I rose into a sky of wilderness,
where I settled on a cloud.

That is where and when I heard your lyric,
like a feather parting leaves of breeze.

Do not redraft your notes.
You are already my Divine music.

When you open,
you pollinate my Purpose.

You exude a thousand shimmering crystals,
all seated in a garden of paradise.

Feed me your manna.

My portions must be gargantuan.
My daily allowance is obscene.

Please, Bride, be excessive with me.

Gush out like a geyser
into the atmosphere of my heart.

Make my cup runneth over.

Surpass all human quotas,
drown me in your syllables of Love.

I met a goatherd once,

in a pasture near the shores
of the Gambia.

He told me of a cave
deep in the Andes,

where ancient scrolls
tell a secret story

of Love's assignment
in the human world.

I went there with a quiet Sherpa
from the loud Himalayan passes.

We searched for weeks,
but never found the cave.

We did find a hermit, though,
chewing on some dark green
medicinal leaves.

He whispered into my ear
an unbelievable legend.

I have not found evidence
of this legend anywhere in the world.

Until now, in this dream with you.

I have to believe that each pulse
of Love inside the souls of humankind,
opens a doorway to a pristine dimension.

Each Love pulse ushers something Holy
to come through that doorway,
increasing Its presence in our realm.

You and I are inviting Light, my Love.

We are swimming in darkness,
drawing phosphorescent spirit.

Our souls in motion
are what attract the Light.

A soul motion known as Love.

Come with me.
Complete this legend.

Unbind its pages.
Set it free.

Beautiful Wife,
come weave this Love with me.

Strip the jungle of its vines.
Encumber me in your affection.

Tie me up to your tree of Passion,
and never cut me loose.

Kidnap my body and all its pulses.
Offer no ransom.

Steal away with me and leave no trail.

Hide me in your burrow.
Seal the opening.

Nest me high in the canopy,
and patrol the skies above.

Keep all others outside
our fierce no-fly zone.

The wisest souls in human history,
in their most brilliant moments,

were fools before the Brilliance
that made you for me.

Your tongue and heart,
mind, soul, and body,

are the petition I sent to God,
before I ever was conceived.

You are the raindrop that perfectly
swallows my thirst.

The feast laid out for my passion,
that leaves me spent and grinning,
soaked in ecstasy.

I want the meadows of fine hair
on your body.

I want the basin of your belly.
Your gaze penetrating my soul.

Explore my coves.
I want your fire. Your dark, rich sap.

Time to leave our formal home.

Tonight, we sleep in the
ceremonial cave,

whose roof is sky,
and whose air and spirit have seen
the most unbelievable things.

My Holy Wife.
I accept your Devotion,

return to you my fealty.
My Matrimonial bond and seal.

I will build for you a castle
of my Servitude.

Present me your primal soul.
I will be its royal bather.

I will be your blacksmith, your horseman,
your court jester, your courtship,

your bathhouse, your well water.
Your feast. Candlelight. Sky.

Your moon, stars, and comets.
Your sunrise and song.

I will be the cricket choir,
strumming you to a soothing sleep,

and the warm strength and brawn,
summoning you awake.

I will be your nighttime companion.
Sentry for your dreams.

My Love, every time you wake
in the night and open your eyes,

my face and form,

and blanket of devotion,
will comfort you.

I pledge my primal heart.
My ancient soul.

I pledge to honor and elevate you.

I pledge to fiercely defend this house,
our single Soul of Love.

I pledge to covet only you.

I pledge to speak Lovingly.
To listen compassionately.

To monsoon your thirst,
and tend your wings.

To honor and encourage
the freedom of your soul,

the joy of your dance,
the fervor of your calling,

and the fulfillment of your life.

I am a leaf.
You are Holy water.

I lay down my life for you.

I have gone to my Sacred lake,

and offered its spirit
my sage and sweet grass.

In the smoke of this offering,
I promise these things to you:

I will plant a thousand wildflowers
of my Love in the soil of your heart

for each moment God grants me
this Union with you.

I will prostrate my identity
before your Beauty,

live as your Greatest Beholder.

I will run up a mountain
to pick you healing herbs
at your slightest ache.

I will dig with my bare hands
in the blistering desert

to find you water
at the first sign
of your sweet lips
running dry.

I will be all that you need me to be.
Give all that I possess.

Fulfill all that you desire.
Manifest all that you ask.

I will be your Prayed for Mate.

For I have always been so.
And can only be so.

Even so,
I choose to be your Mate for life.

Kiss me deeply,

and I will take you finally
into this picturesque terrain of Love.

Now we begin our bliss,
and live inside our Love Eternity.

My lips rest softly upon thee.

My body is your dowry.
My heart your entitlement.

My soul your endowment.

My life and breath,
the garden for your heart's
pleasure and pronunciation.

With each pulse of your existence,
I am wedding you once more.

I consummate this Love with you
upon the soft bright meadow
of our Merging.

With my body,
I enter the aching song of your desire,

and sing with you the Heavenly sound
of our single Soul.

Wed me today with your passion.

If I cannot kiss my Love
across your shoreline,

my heart will rupture.

My Love is a forge
that will not stop roaring.

Take me to your landscape.
We have all day.

Arch your Glory.
Be my pleasure's gateway.

Moan your meaning.

Let me fill you past paradise,
into nirvana's Greatest dream.

Wildflowers are showing us
what must be done.

We will merge into the woods.
Join with the moss.

And our pleasure will call forth
all living things.

Please, share your grain with me.

Among billions of souls on earth,

it is your regard
that matters to me.

You are my standard.
My perspective.

I orient my sails
by the compass of your mood.

You are my joyful priority,
my perpetuity, my life of praise.

Whatever I pour into you,
appreciates in spirit value.

I am dashed to the stars
upon the comet trails of this Love.

You kill all that I was,
and resurrect all that I am meant to be.

You do such supernatural things to me.

My Holy Provision.

My Gift of a Great God's
Hospitality.

I will.

I will marry you.

I stand upon Mount Sinai
in a brilliant black night,

sky sparkling with rivers of lightning,
resounding with roars of thunder.

I am a divining rod soaked with Purpose.

Holiness arcs Its Electricity
toward my being

in Fateful fingers
that dance and illuminate the dark.

I am entered by Creation,
splintered by Intent.

Upon the tablets of my tender heart
and helpless soul,

the Commandment of my lifetime
is inscribed in an unearthly Fire:

LOVE THIS SOUL.
LOVE THIS WOMAN.

LOVE HER AS YOU LOVE ME,
YOUR MAKER.

RECEIVE AND BECOME
HER LOVE FOR YOU,

WHICH IS MY LOVE FOR YOU.

AND THROUGH THIS SINGULAR
SOUL OF LOVE,

THIS TRIUMPHANT
FLOWER OF UNION,

BEAR MY LIGHT IN THE WORLD.

CAPTIVATE THE DARKNESS
OF HUMANKIND.

DASH THE DIMNESS
OF A FEARFUL HORDE.

BRIGHTEN MY CREATION
IN YOUR AWESOME SONG OF LOVE.

WAKE THE DANCE
OF MY BELOVED CHILDREN.

OPEN THE ARCHIVES
OF THEIR GODLY LOVE.

LET FAITH RISE AGAIN
AS THE SUMMER SUN.

BURN AWAY
THESE AGES OF APATHY.

IGNITE PRAISE AND WORSHIP
IN THE MOMENTARY EXISTENCE
OF YOUR KIND.

LET YOUR LOVE BE MY SALVE
AND PROMISE TO THE WORLD.

RECALL THE ANGELS.
OPEN THE ATTIC TO HEAVEN.

ENTICE HUMAN DESIRE
TO TURN ITS PALTRY DREAMS

TOWARD THE ENDLESS OCEAN
OF MY LOVE.

BE WHAT I AM,

TO ENLIST WHAT I COMMAND
OF EVERY SOUL:

TO BE MY LOVE.

I GIVE UNTO YOU THIS
RAPTUROUS CHARGE.

LOVE THIS SOUL.

HOUSE THIS WOMAN IN THE LOVE
AND MATRIMONY FOR WHICH

I HAVE ENVISIONED
AND THEREFORE CREATED YOU.

BE HER LATITUDE AND
LONGITUDE.

BE HER LIFETIME OF LOVE.

And so, yes,
sweet and Sacred Love.

I will.

I will marry you.

Explode into Light.
Enter my soul in luminosity.

Union may only happen
when two objects are in a state of light.

Light makers are Love makers.

I retire from this life.
You are my sole vocation and calling.

For, any true calling can only be fulfilled
through Love's Spirit.

I am so alive and euphoric.

Grace pours such an Infinite
blessing into our soul.

Hallelujah.
Hallowed be our Love.

Still and always,

you make my soul
cry gratitude.

I *choose you* to be the monument
of my Love in this world.

As you grow and nurture your soul,
I will polish what you have grown.

Oceans of Love tears
continue to rise from my abyssal center.

I bring them to this polishing.

Please take me inside your garden,
let me mist you like rain.

I am bowed and broken.

I kiss the feet of Holiness,
and weep unto the Sky of skies.

For I am found in you.

My every remaining breath
shall be of Gratitude.

With my heart and soul,
I will build your home.

And you will be wanted
more than you have known wanting.

A wanting that torches your chains,
and sets you at last...

to your Intended Peace.

We wed, not for our sake,
but for the sake of Love's prophecies.

The Tree of Life is consumed
with spreading its branches.

We are its fruit. Its fulfillment.

Behold its tears of sap
as it beholds our sap of Love.

Only one way out for Spirit
in this tangible territory:

through Union's multiplicity.

Through the repetition of our touch,
touch of body, of feeling, of soul.

What is this fire?
Into what volcano have I been dropped?

In my chest, I can feel the rumors
of an old magma as it rises through
my shafts and corridors.

A geyser builds that will not be polite.

Its force shall level this valley
of timid romances.

Only a crater will remain.

A great, steaming earth depression,
soon filled with sacred water.

Do you understand, Sweet Dream,
that as you radiate your desire,

you metamorphose my crust
into molten dissolution?

You bring me to boil at a glance,
touch me into fluidity

that fits through spaces
my rigidness could not before.

I was an island that never could
quite grasp the looming distant shore.

You have made me water,
fluid and free.

Now, I can reach
that Forevermore.

I am so broken and crumbled
before the Supernatural Gift
of your soul and our Love.

You have resurrected my Fulfillment
and Joy on Earth.

You are my Perfect Medicine.

I will Love you with all that I am,
forever, and my every remaining breath
shall be Thanksgiving and celebration.

I am but a cloud.
You are my endless sky.

You illuminate and enrapture
my life and soul.

I choose you.

I wed you endlessly,
with every pulse and beat
of Creation.

You have distilled me
into my secret dialect.

I am nothing but Love code.

You are my destination.

I have been homeless and obtuse
all of these years.

Your heart dashes my shutters.
You brighten me impossibly.

Let me move into you,
and open all your soul's windows.

I will take such good care of you.

Your Light will be amplified
unto the world,

and within our private fluttering.

Soul whom I Love,
let me enter you and remain forever.

Love, you are my poet.
I will never stop falling into your pages.

Nor can I quench this thirst
for your fine pronunciation,
your eloquent way of existence.

No world except this world with you.

Give me a vacant treehouse.
Just furnish it with your scent,

and locate it high in the canopy,
beyond the reach of unsatisfied souls,

and their inclement weather.

High and unreachable,
inside a sacred mist of Love.

You are my endless meteor shower
in the spectacular sky of our intimacy.

My Song.
My Worship Dance.

Nothing exists but as a reflection of you.
Everything exists in you.

God collapsed Creation
into the bud you are,

and bid you to bloom inside of me.

I taste all generations in you.

In you, I catch the scent
of every Love story, of every yearning.

Oh, I am burning.
This is no tidy composing.

I write this naked in a thunderous rain.

I write this in the aggressive desert,
my skin at the mercy of sun.

I write this in a den of cubs.
Soaked in Jordan's river.

Blazing on a pyre.

This Love, so abrupt and rampaging.
So sublime and seeping.

I am on the moon, drinking its glow,
my lips in its tidal belly.

The jungle of my desire takes me.

Roots and vines invade my courtyard,
split my foundation.

This robust ecology
breaks and enters my windows.

I am the breeze that follows inside.

Close the doors.
Board the windows.
Shutter Creation.

You are my Existence.

I am a comet. Ice and dust
melting across your atmospheres.

You touch me with a finger of Love,
and my glaciers shrug and surrender
into your warming sea.

My heart is a ripe pomegranate,
a billion seeds burgeoning and bursting,

its flesh diaphanous
and wearing skirts of light,
hemmed in desire,

organic cotton
pulled from its bed and thorn,

bleeding to be made
into your lifelong blanket,
your daily warmth against all chills.

I do not compose this.

It erupts from my Truth
in torrents of clouds and mist,
of sand dissolved into air.

You are a single grass
I graze for eternity.

Wild berries
ripened by moon.

Put me in the field,

let me pick you from dawn to midnight,
with no break, no respite.

You are my respite.
This world is my labor.

I spill my Love and wade in the lagoon
your soul is for me.

I am the song in the trees
you hear when morning breaks.

You break my heart into sweet rain.
Into God sounds.

Into Love.

No more words,
just this access to your heart.

No more world,
just this privacy with your desire.

No more No's and Yes's,
just this Proof of life
that is my Love for you.

I am the willow branches dancing.
Your soul, this wind, my irresistible music.

Arch your beauty into my obsession.
Make me.

You are my precious sun.
I wake only to behold your Sacred beauty.

I sleep to sort through dreams,

until I find the ones
where your flower grows.

I am not a man who Loves.

I am Love,
who has been sent a woman.

You are my bird of paradise.

I am your colors, in Love,
that flood through you.

Then, you become the flood in me.

I have wandered,

a Love monk pilgrimaging
through pueblos and reservations,

asking for mercy, and for word of you.

Kind souls sat me at their
long, wooden tables,

brought me green chilé stew
to warm my bones,

and pasolé and frijoles
to fortify my brittleness.

I drank their sweet milk
of rice and cinnamon,

nutmeg and cloves,
vanilla and sugar.

And when the ripe moon
appeared through the window,
casting the room in supernatural light,

they invited me by the fire,
and, in circle, with drum and dusk,

shared with me the legend of a woman
learned about as children, at the knees of
their old ones.

She was known as
Water In Her Eyes.

Creator had shaped her
from red rock, willow leaves,
and cottonwood bark.

She was made to have a porous soul.

A soul that Spirit entered more easily
and often than with other souls.

Spirit World flowed into her,
and through her, with every breath.

All living things were drawn to her,

drawn by the medicine water
they could smell and sense in her.

As Creation poured through her
continuously, she was touched deeply
by Its pure spirit.

Because of this, she cried often.

Animals made her cry.
Memories brought tears.

Small delights, like a single sand grain,
caused her heart to flush and flood.

Everywhere she went,
streams of water were left behind.

Fresh water.

This was useful in the desert.

Water In Her Eyes
was the reason that so many
families and communities
were able to survive.

The people who shared
her legend with me,

always spoke of her reverently,
tenderly.

They also told me that
I, too, was a water spirit.

And that, one day, I would meet her.

Solace, Sanctity, I know she is you.

Before, I existed in quicksand.

Then, one night,
I felt a Spectacular mating
fuse my soul and spirit with yours.

The next morning, air had become water.
I could breathe in your element.

I was free and swimming.

You were my blood.
I was your breath.

I pray you will always pour your water.
And make all things new.

Sacred Wife.
Holder of my Heart.
Fortress of my Love and Life.

Thank you for washing me
in your Loving words.

You are a hummingbird,
drinking from the hibiscus blossom.

You are my hibiscus blossom.
I come to drink from you.

Please know the power
of your words with me.

With your breath,
you can destroy my existence,
and also bear unto me new life.

Only you possess such Potency of Word.

Your soul is my cathedral.
Your words my sermon.

You are the Poetry
of which I have been dreaming.

I need no other script.

Give me your Poetry,
and I will give you my life.

Together, an otherworldly Garden.

My Love is the root
winding around your lyric tree.

Don't release me.
Grow. Incorporate me.

One single flower will ever grow
in the meadow of my soul.

You. You. You.
Always and only you.

You are the sweetest blossom
I have touched or held.

I am water vapor,
belonging to your sky.

Only there can I rain down on earth
the fullness of this Love that I am.

I am a lemon on a tree,
so ripe and ready for you.

Pick me.
Have your way.

Stir my fruit in the sweet water of Grace.
Drink me into your being.

I want to sprout from your soil
as a field of your favorite flowers,

and encumber you in my petals

as you drift to sleep.

Lie upon me forever.
Grow with me.

Become with me the sound of Bliss.
The wind chime of Glory.

Become with me the sweet fragrance
in the air that heals this world,

and takes all souls home to Love.

Precious Love.

You are my sky and meadow.
My sweet brook and sunrise.

My spirit is stronger,
purer than my body.

Do not live in the security of
my bodily presence.

Live in the assurance
of my spiritual ever-presence.

You are never alone.

We are spirit wed.
Melded and fused.

Formed together
and still each free, free, free.

My entirety turns toward you.

You are the gravity for which I fall.
The atmosphere in which I burn.

The current that takes me.
Take me home.

Convene the poets of antiquity.

Only old language
can pour this fresh spring water.

All the new language
is still traveling the circle
to meet its Maker.

You are a mountain spring,
sweet and fresh and clear,

pouring your goodness Faithfully.

I put my mouth to the brook,
drinking.

What enters is alpine.
Filtered through ages
of rocks and sediment.

So clean,
even the ancestors within me
are washed and purified.

What was prayed forth, came forth,
and the world was beautiful again.

You are streams of light and laughter,
orchards lush with ripest caring fruit.

You are eagle, seeing deeply
into the soul of sky and earth.

Joy laid out on a meadow,
with a book, and paradise
floating through.

You are born. You live.

And because you live,
the world is beautiful again.

You want to see what mountains see,
to witness the eagle's view.

Let what spirit I possess
take wing and lift you there.

May I have your kind permission
to help you heal?

If I may,
I will add what ingredient I can,
to dissolve your childhood bindings,

your years of wounds and scars
from the cactus touch of suffering ones.

If you will, I volunteer to hold open
the heavy corral gate,

while you break away to freedom.
Always to freedom.

Peace has a taste like plantains.
Or peaches.

Except the Peace you finally find,
that will taste like a profound recipe.

The kind you prepare as you walk
this world in your true form:

tender-hearted Light.

I have not heard a word
this world has spoken
since your spirit first spoke to me.

I have been consumed
in cherishing your natural beauty,

your naked face
that no manmade contrivance
can hope to improve.

You have already had
the only makeover
worthy of your radiance.

You were *made over* at conception,
into your form in this world.

Since then, you have been
the luminosity of Divine perfection.

When you look in the mirror,

you see flaws.

When I look into the mirror
that is your heavenly face,

I see the ultimate appearance
of Love Itself.

In the morning, you cannot be
more beautiful, more glowing to me.

Angels glisten on your skin.
Your spirit has not yet returned to earth.

You are untouched by man's idea of you.

Unblemished by your own self-Love
gone astray.

In that moment, you are
your original beauty.

Unsurpassable. Organic. Free.

You wake, and you are whole and finished.

Please, do not disrobe your essence.
Don't mask your true face.

I want you.

Not a concoction taught to you
by a world of concocted personas.

Please, I will have the clay
fresh from its Maker.

The bread fresh from the Oven of clay.

You need no makeup.
You were already made. Up. There.

Bring *that* down here, with me.

Let Love praise Love.

Promise me we will live prostrated,

our knees in the soil,
hearts pleading and plaintive.

Like this, we can farm kindness
from the fallow ground of this
world's infertile way of life.

Like this, we can offer warm meals
to the holy masses,

and pour drink that soothes
the deeper belly and bones

of so many who only want
to be humanly regarded.

Come make this Love with me.

I have seen large fish,
their bodies nearly out of the water,

grazing moss from rocks,
and strands of hanging leaves.

Anyone who dares leave her element
to taste what grows just beyond,
finds uncommon blessings.

You are one of those.

I have seen you grazing paradise.

Now, you taste like frosting
on a cake of Light.

I admire the way you behave like rainbows,
expressing your flush and fever
so publicly.

No wonder you sleep so deeply.

You are retrieving a world of color
back into your jar.

Speaking of sleep,
may I borrow your belly tonight?

My face against it sleeps
the way winter sleeps through June.

Purge the mistresses of this life,

the infernal distractions that promise
pleasure, yet evaporate coldly,

leaving not emptiness,
for emptiness is a gift of space,

but rather disillusionment,

which feels like days given away.
Like dreams prostituted for crumbs.

Purge the inventory of my wastefulness.
Destroy the levies, flood the canals.

I want to be rushed through
with the bright water that matters.

Woman, make my channels useful again.

No more barges and bloated flotillas
captained by drunks and greed.

Only the purity of a paper boat,
folded by a child,

and set to sail by Hope,
caught in the wind
of your attention,

your soul leaning
in the same direction
of the servitude that I seek.

I want my entire ocean
inside of every suffering creek.

Meet me at that delta.

Furnish those estuaries with your
vibrant species of empathy.

Let's grow whole new wetlands,

marshes and swamps to fortress
the coastlines of this humanity,

to keep us all from the surge of
storms churned up from the deep
of suffering's brethren.

Let our sunrise open human eyes
to the web of life spun by Eternity.

I am flagrant
with my nakedness.

I don't care who sees.

Tear off your clothes
and join me in this rapture.

Let them jail us
for indecency.

I am tired of this supposed freedom.

It is no more than another
uninspired breed of jail.

No moon shines through these bars.
Only platonic dusk, so timid.

Walking hand in hand
is a gift that mocks us.

Walking soul in soul
is a truer closeness.

My shoulders glisten
in this raging light.

Such is the labor necessary
to birth your untouched ecstasy.

Meet me by the water.

Scorpion's sting
has already killed my inhibition.

I go now to soak my storm
in the roiling currents.

Meet me there.
We'll go under.
Come up gasping.

Roaring. Rolling.

Show me your true form.

Let me awe and open
my anterior chamber.

Even forests blush
when they see us
dewing what we do.

For us, the sand today.
I am inspired to create a mandala.

A sacred symbol that ushers us deeper,
even as it lifts us out into the universe.

We must practice our openness
in such small and ceremonial ways.

Healthy relationships are not enclosures.
They are open spaces.

Life grows in that greenhouse,
showered in the sunlight of truthfulness.

This is what you bring me, daily.

Your truth shorn of its winter coat,
its layers of protection.

I am so humbled to earn the delicacy,
the truth that is your nakedness.

Human souls are porous.

Easily moved by the spirit of wilderness
and its pristine breath.

Walk with me these many hillsides,

breathing the scent of wild sage
and rain-freshened lavender.

Walk with me, chewing sweet grass,

through the ballet of butterflies
and ruby-throated sparrows.

The air up at the mountain pass
drums with unreal gusts,

is so clean that to breathe it,
is to breathe your own rebirth.

Lie with me under the oaks,
on the moss-blanketed earth.

Let our words go wandering.
Like children, they will come back.

For now, this silence, this stillness
that rings through the soul,

a monastery bell
high in the aspen alpines,
resonating your heartbeat
and mine to calm.

And then to sleep.

Remember when we splashed
in the turquoise lagoon?

The water was unreal that day.
Something mineral soaked our skin.

We kissed under the spiraling waterfall,
lost all sense of separation.

We became one water, falling.
One water, pooling, flowing.

Day left us a blanket of sun,
on which we lay and sighed.

And when we left turquoise lagoon,

your dreams had crossed over
into the landscape of my chest.

Since then, when your soul stirs,
its stirring wakes inside of me.

When you want honey,
I am already at the hive.

At your first glance,
my ice age retreated.

A verdant valley sprung up,
with all its forms of beauty.

Now, I live my life
in a state of tethered pleasure.

I am tied to you, yet unbound.
Inhale such freedom.

I cannot be more alive.
Not for the life of me.

In quiet moments,
on our broad porch
overlooking Creation,

I Love the feel of breeze
on my skin,

skin that wants profound affection
with this reality.

And I Love the touch
of your hand as it drifts down
and settles on my arm,

a leaf that Love's tree
drops so caringly.

Take off your clothes.

It is time for us to wade
in the healing waters,

in the gulfs and bays

eroded and unprotected.

Through our Love,
we will sow seeds
in the thinned out reeds,

and rebuild the soft and sturdy
growth that insulates continents
from ice ages of the soul.

It is time for you and me
to wade in the healing waters,

deep and up to our necks
in coastal tides,

where mothers and fathers
wash their children, clothes, and dishes,

wash their pains and memories,
wash residue of their humanity.

If we wade deeply,
our bodies insulated by our intimacy,

we can plant these seeds deep enough,
to withstand the gales of despair,
and grow to maturity.

We are not given this Love for our sake,

but to be a mirror for those who wander
invisible through days of nights,

never glancing the possibility
of their own Love Creation.

Our human family is losing the scent
of the sustenance we track.

Only souls dissolved in Grace
can get us back.

Oh, the mercury of the road
we humans walk,

the shepherds and their flocks,
the quiet women and men

tending their chores
of spiritual dimension,

and the malodorous spirits
who usher us falsely.

Get out the blueprints.
We will build a new palace.

Two souls aligned in Sacred harmony

can and do become conduits
to the plains of Grace.

and who else to share the bread,
and pour the water,
than true Lovers,

who have been baked
and purified in the ovens
and filtration of a Holiness
beyond nations?

Your carnal passion, my Love,
is the appetite of True Passion.

My bodily desire, a flicker
in the flames of True Fire.

We are sculpting a staircase
to the Sky,

even as we are being shaped
as useful clay.

Our wanting is the way to Glory.

For, our Lovemaking
is the making of Holy Love.

Making it in this world,
drawn from the World of worlds,

poured out here in this desert,
this life, this human striving.

When you look at me,
your soul arrives at the soul of me,

and then at the Soul that sets me free.

As I burn for you,
I burn for Entirety.

Our Love wakes a flower.

That flower is medicine for suffering
and pilgrimage to Hope.

A line has been thrown down
from the high clouds.

Let us grab that mystic rope.

And climb this miracle,

along the prenatal buds
of our moments,

which birth our moments.

Which birth our Love.

Jaiya John was born and raised in New Mexico, and has lived in various locations, including Nepal. He serves his life purpose through relationship, writing, speaking, and supporting young lives. He is the founder of Soul Water Rising, a global human mission.

Jacqueline V. Richmond and Kent W. Mortensen graciously and skillfully served as editors for *Habanero Love*.

Jaiya John titles are available where books are sold. Book revenue supports our *Young Life Drumbeat* youth development programming, including our scholarship and book donation programs for displaced and vulnerable youth.

Other Books by Jaiya John

To learn more about this and other books by Jaiya John, to order discounted bulk quantities, or to learn about Soul Water Rising's global work, please visit us at:

soulwater.org

jaiyajohn.com

facebook.com/jaiyajohn

itunes (search: jaiya john)

youtube.com/soulwaterrising

@jaiyajohn (Instagram & twitter)

To subscribe to our literary journal, *SOUL BLOSSOM*, please visit soulwater.org.

Soul Blossom is a literary journal, offering ongoing news of our global human mission, new book release notices, speaking engagement insights, and invited literary contributions.

Soul Blossom is also a gathering space for the writing and artwork of young people from around the world.

CPSIA information can be obtained
at www.ICGtesting.com
Printed in the USA
BVHW030033080221
599518BV00008B/1198

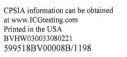

9 780991 640157